FACING
THE STORM

Meditations and Prayers
by
Eddie Askew

By the same author:

A Silence and a Shouting
Disguises of Love
Many Voices One Voice
No Strange Land
Breaking the Rules
Cross Purposes

1989

4th Impression 1996

ISBN 0 902731 30 0

Photoset and printed by Stanley L. Hunt (Printers) Ltd, Rushden, Northants

For Samuel Thomas Hawke:
too young to know yet,
but the future gets closer
each day.

Cover picture from a watercolour by the author

Foreword

THE sensitivity, freshness and acute insight of Eddie Askew's devotional books have aroused great appreciation, and in response he has now written a fifth volume. The series of meditations and prayers originated in his monthly pastoral letters to Leprosy Mission colleagues worldwide, and each collection is enhanced by the author's own pencil drawings.

Eddie Askew has given 37 years of service to leprosy sufferers, spending 15 years in India with his wife Barbara, and latterly directing The Leprosy Mission International until his retirement.

Canada Geese

Matthew 6:25-27

IT was cold, down at the nature reserve. The sky was steel grey, clouds torn by an almost gale-force wind. It ripped through the trees, scattering the last leaves. The water was grey and ruffled. A great armada of Canada geese was in the water, together with dozens of other waterbirds. They all floated there, facing into the storm.

Their environment had suddenly become hostile, threatening. They didn't protest, or run for cover. They didn't use up precious energy flying into it, or fighting it. They faced into the wind, paddling quietly. They didn't try to make headway, but paddled just enough to keep their direction and position in the water.

Maybe we can learn from the birds. Jesus thought so. They tell us of God's concern, he said, and remind us that we achieve little by worrying.

When the going gets tough, the tough get going, says the cliché. I'm not sure that's always the best way. We're not all as aggressive as that suggests. Another way is just to face the storm, and keep position. Not scream and shout, not protest and ask what have I done to deserve this, but just hold on to faith and wait for the wind to blow itself out. It will, because the creator of the winds is stronger than the wind.

It may take time, but it works, and I don't remember ever seeing a Canada goose with acute depression.

Look at the birds.
That's what you said, Lord.

And there they are,
just getting on
with the business of living.
Being birds.
Facing the storm.

That's part of my problem, I reckon.
Not content to be me.
Wanting something different.
Creating my own tensions.
Piling up the building blocks of discontent.
Making my own high-rise apartments of unhappiness.
Isolating myself in anxiety.
Made worse
when the hand of reality
gives it all a push,
and I sit,
a child in the ruins,
howling.

Help me understand, Lord,
that wherever I'm at,
you're there.
That you have something for me.
That you care.
As a hen gathers her chicks under her wings,
you said.

Nice picture, that.
Safe from the world,
warm, secure.
But chicks grow up,
and so must I.
Get out into the cold wind
of the world out there.

But knowing that your wings
are stronger than the storm.

I think I can live with that.

Psalm 46

A CHURCH minister was being interviewed on television. His wife had been a deacon in the Anglican Church. She had died, just two weeks earlier. The day she was ordained she had been told that she had leukaemia. "After the initial shock," he said, "She made it clear that she didn't agree with God about it".

I warmed to that. Our discipleship shouldn't make us unthinking zombies, accepting everything that happens without question. We have a right, even a duty, to use the minds God gave us. Not simply to repeat the well-worn platitudes.

"Did prayer help?" he was asked. A thoughtful pause. "Yes ... but don't ask me how. Prayer is learning to rest in God."

Resting in God. After the questioning, and not necessarily getting the answer you want, or think you need, resting in him is all there is. Leaving it with him, even when we disagree. Relying on his love.

I get less and less satisfied with the sort of prayer that's constant petition. Of course asking is part of prayer, but it tends to take over. I suspect it's the activist in us — we want things done, decisions made, goals accomplished.

But in the end, the relationship between God and me has to go beyond that — to resting. Learning simply to sit with him, quietly. Leaving the final decisions with him. They're his anyway, and if he's not competent to deal with them, nobody is.

Lord, if it's questions you want
I've got them.
Bucketsful.
I'm like someone just out of depth,
standing on tiptoe,
the tide sucking away the sand
from under my feet.
My arms stretched out,
just above the waterline of doubt.
The water's cold,
it slaps my face.
Another wave and I'll go under.

But when I pause,
take breath, so shakily,
I think, perhaps if I asked less
there'd be more time
to hear your answers.
My mind's so full
of self-created doubts
there's little space for you.

Part of the trouble, Lord,
is that I want life tidy.
Secure. Predictable.
And that's not how you work.
I've found that out,
painfully at times.
I've got the scars to prove it.
But occasionally I find the honesty
to say that you're in charge.

And so I ask, Lord,
not necessarily to understand
the way things are,
but just to find the grace
to rest in you.
To let my problems wait.
To still my mind
and in the blessed peace and quiet
that comes when I relax,
and lift my arms,
surrender to your presence.
And in your nearness
find that's all I need.

Matthew 25:14-30

"YOU have talent," said someone, looking at some pictures I'd painted recently, "That's a great gift".

It is, and I thank God for it almost every day. The trouble is, that while people admire the "gift" — artistic or otherwise — they tend to assume it's something given to you fully developed. More like a present.

It isn't. The artist with the greatest talent is usually the one who works hardest. The painter with the big London exhibition is often one who works compulsively, sacrificing everything else to it. His talent is the basis on which he builds the rest, and he won't succeed without it, but it remains latent until he starts to use it. Without the practice, the discipline, and the sweat, the talent is only a promise. It's developed by working on it.

The gift becomes greater as it's exercised. There's the story of a painter who dashed off a lovely little sketch in a dozen strokes of his brush. It had life and vigour and beauty. "How long did it take you to do that?" asked an admirer, expecting to be told, "Ten minutes". "30 years," answered the painter, thinking of all the experience that had gone into it.

Jesus offers us a new sort of life, a new vision of truth. But he doesn't offer it on a plate, like a free gift with 20 litres of petrol. He asks us to work at it.

Lord, I understand,
that what you've given me
is meant to be developed.

I understand.
Which isn't the same
as saying I like it.
I'd prefer life ready-made.
Bought off the peg.
A reasonable fit, but cheap.
Nothing too demanding.
A holiday cruise,
full of colour and romance,
but air-conditioned from the heat
of commitment.
What you ask sometimes seems
more like a seat in a galley.
Rowing hard against the tide,
and sometimes into danger.

A little exercise,
a little love,
a little bit of giving,
is one thing — or three, to be exact —
but your demands are so much more.
You ask my life and time,
my mind and heart.
You're never satisfied with less.
It seems a bit unreasonable, Lord.
Too much for you to ask,
or me to give.

But then, Lord, I acknowledge
that your demands are made in love.
That in its fertile ground
my roots can spread
and grow up to maturity.
That what you offer me
isn't the grind of soulless self-denial,
but the affirmation of my being.
That in the contradictory freedom
that your service brings,
I can be so much more
than I ever was before.
I find I'm rich with talents
I never knew I had,
whether through laziness or lack of consciousness
I'm never sure.

And I can live beyond myself.

Lord, help me step out
in fearful faith today.
Ready to use my energies for you.
In hope.
In confidence.
With joy.

Windsor Castle

John 1:1-9

THE morning service had just begun. It was the third Sunday in Advent, and two of the children went forward and lit the Advent candles. From the pew behind me a little boy was keeping up a barrage of questions to granny. Finally, as the children went back to their seats, he asked loudly, "Who's going to blow the candles out?"

I suppose his only experience of candles was on his birthday cake, when he'd been encouraged to blow them out in one big breath. That, he thought, was the only thing to do with candles.

The words in John's gospel came to me: "The light shines in the darkness, but the darkness has not overcome it".

Not for want of trying. It seems at times as though all the powers of the world are trying to put out the light Jesus brought, and that they'd think it was a birthday celebration if they succeeded. But weak though it seems, the candle flame of love flickers on, dispelling the darkness around it, ready to ignite new lights wherever there is faith and commitment.

Why should it be like that? Why is there such opposition? An alternative translation says "... but the darkness has not understood it". The light looks like a threat. It frightens, shows up the things we'd rather have hidden. Disturbs us.

We don't understand that the truth is different. That light promises life, freedom, and an end to fear. The irony is that we have to find the courage to affirm it before the fear can be dealt with. The courage to make a leap of faith through the darkness towards that candle flame of love. But is it really such a risk? It burns with all the power of God, and it's been burning for a long time, in spite of all the huffing and puffing of the world.

Lord, there are moments
when it seems
that darkness has the upper hand.
Light burns dim,
only a flickering candle
blown sideways by capricious storms.
Clouds roll in,
the sheepdog wind herding them tightly,
penning them beyond the limits of my sight.
Their shadows race across my meadow.
The air bites chill.
The picnic's over.

Sometimes the darkness
welcomes me.
Embraces,
hides my imperfections,
masks my sin,
from everyone but me,
and you.
Holds me clamped tight
lest I reach out to you.

"And darkness covered the earth."
Covered it twice, Lord.
First, at creation,
when you brought order out of chaos.
Gave life and light.
Then at the re-creation of the world.
Signed by the cross.
Darkness triumphant,
or so it seemed
for one brief pause.
Then, in confused retreat,
before the risen Lord of life and light.

Shine in my darkness, Lord.
Dispel the doubt and fear
that cling so close.
Turn the weak moonlight of my faith
to brighter day
in which I see your radiance,
know your love.

Mark 4:30-32

I'M fascinated by bonsai trees. Bonsai is an ancient tradition, begun by the Chinese hundreds of years ago, and later developed by the Japanese. You take small tree seedlings and, by a combination of root restriction and careful pruning, produce miniature trees.

They're just like the real thing, but dwarf. In China and Japan I've seen pine trees, 100 years old, gnarled and weathered, only two feet tall. Japanese maples perfect in scale, but only a few inches high. A whole grove of beech trees arranged in a flat ceramic tray less than a yard across. Many of them are breathtakingly beautiful. They become heirlooms, handed down through the family.

It's fine as long as we're talking about trees. The trouble is we sometimes do it to our faith. We confine its roots, restrict its growth, keep it miniature. We can become bonsai-believers, our timidity holding us within a tiny and familiar environment. We refuse ourselves — and others — the freedom to branch out, to grow up and develop. We are happy to keep our roots in the small pot of our own tradition, confined to comfortable routine.

Jesus said the kingdom of God is like a grain of mustard seed. A tiny seed which grows into a great tree with room for all the birds to perch. Let's rejoice in its growth, the bigger the better, and not try to restrict it to our own little experience.

A grain of seed, Lord.
Tiny. Inert.
The tight-turned, curled embryo
held hard within.
Straitjacketed by winter waiting.
Yet in your purposes
destined for life and growth.
Ready to reach for light,
expand, spread branches.
Leaf, bud, and fruit.

The kingdom of heaven,
like a grain of seed.
The kingdom of heaven, in me.
Its seed tight-packed.
Restricted in the shell of my inertia.
The warmth of your Spirit
prompts it to life.
But when it stirs,
sets root, and starts to grow,
I hold it back.
I feel its movement apprehensively.
I can't see your purposes.
My horizon is too small and limited
because I keep my head too low,
look down too much.
I prune and chop
and starve your kingdom's tree,
hoping to hold it,
controlled and tidy,
in a little pot of my own choosing.

But still it grows.
Pushing its gentle way irresistibly
between the hard stones of my life.

Lord, help me to sweep away
the sand of fear
blown, hard and persistently,
heaping unbelief in drifts across my life.
Help me to feel
in the prompting of new growth,
the excitement, the hope and tension,
of your Spirit's purposes.
And when I don't understand
just where it's leading to,
help me to welcome it.

1 Corinthians 3:16-19

BEHIND the carved oak pulpit in the old church, I noticed a mark on the worn wall. At first glance, I thought it was just a random roughness, a shadow on the stone. Then I realised it was the outline of a cross. It must have hung there for years and, when taken down, it left the mark on the wall.

As individual Christians we leave a mark. Most of us lead unremarkable lives. Actually, I'm not so sure of that. When you get to know people you find few who are "ordinary". No-one is exactly like another. Each is remarkable in individual experience. Each of us has something of value to give. But we lead unspectacular lives, rarely producing headlines in the newspapers. Yet our presence in the world, our faithful performance of the little acts of daily living, makes its mark.

There are times when we feel useless. We can't stop the steamroller of world events without getting flattened. No-one listens to the thin sound of our protest. But "your living shall not be in vain", as the song puts it. We make our mark and, however small it is, it's our mark, and the world will never be quite the same again.

God grant the mark we leave is the mark of the cross.

Lord, I find it hard
to believe it matters,
the little mark
I make on the world.
I'm so caught up
in things I can't control.
Can't even understand the problem
half the time.
I feel lost,
swallowed up,
my efforts useless.

If I stand out in the storm,
waving my little leaf of protest,
it's quickly whipped away,
wind-blighted, seared.
And nothing seems to change.
At times,
I think I hear
an echo of unpleasant laughter,
far away.

I get the feeling
there's nothing I can do.
And not much point in trying.

Yet in the quiet,
I still feel that inner sense,
which I can only say is you,
urging me on.
Telling me,
however small I am,
or weak,
you care for what I do.
Reminding me, so gently,
that however small a mark I make,
it's mine, and yours.
And telling me
to do the little thing
in front of me, today.

I may not see
its cosmic breadth,
or deep significance —
sounds pompous anyway —
but in the faithful living out
and quiet affirmation

of this day's duty,
lies worth, and joy.
And on some wall
a mark is made.
A mark of love,
shaped like a cross.

Old Elms

Mark 10:13-16

CHRISTMAS is a cross and a woolly hippopotamus. Or so it seemed the other Sunday.

My home church is housed in a modern building — a church in the round. The pews are set in three-quarters of a circle, and the focal point is the communion table. Usually, a cross, a Bible and a small bowl of flowers stand on the table. Nothing else. For Communion services, of course, there's bread and wine. Simple and uncluttered.

This morning was different. The table was almost covered, the cross nearly obscured. There were two woolly hippos, several dolls, a family of teddy bears, a furry rabbit, boxes, books and crayons. It was a *Toy Service*, and the toys were gifts from the congregation to a local centre helping children with mental handicap.

On the table woolly hippos, or bread and wine? It seemed an incongruous contrast at first sight. But below the superficial difference, I felt a deeper similarity. Both were expressions of love, both made the incarnation a reality. Both pointed to the truth that God cares, that he stands with the weak and vulnerable.

Sometimes theology seems so abstract and remote, yet the reality of love is simple and concrete. And can be expressed as well in a woolly hippo as in anything else.

Lord, sometimes it seems
we try to keep you safe
in some old echoing museum of theology.
We hold you,
treasured but remote.
We dust the showcase,
occasionally renew the label.
Show our respect in regular visits,
Sunday by Sunday,
the only contact with the world outside
the flower arrangements.
Tastefully done.

But you are Lord of life,
not some old image of Victorian conformity.
You brim with energy,
with the urgency of now.
Your word calls me
to make contact with today.
Challenges my preconceptions.
Faces me with the world
that lies outside
the double-glazed and insulated walls
of my religion.
Confronts me with the call to love,
not abstract ideas,
but people.

Your cross was wood from a living tree,
real blood, real pain.
And you call me to follow you
into that world.
To show my love in ordinary ways,
to ordinary people.
Help me, Lord,
never to lose touch
with your reality.
Help me to see
compassion in a teddy bear,
an image of your love,
in toys freely given.

John 8:31-36

I WAS asked recently to spend a couple of days taking photographs in a hospital for people with mental handicaps. With good training, and proper support, many can go back into society and lead fulfilling lives. The photographs would be used to explain this to the public.

Before I went there, I'd thought vaguely, when I'd bothered to think at all, that this rehabilitation was just another attempt to cut the number and cost of those under care. Now I see differently.

In the art therapy department, I watched a man cutting pictures out of a mail order catalogue to stick on paper as a collage. The choice of pictures was his. He'd covered the paper with "home" symbols — easy chairs, a bedroom, kitchen furniture. It showed what was important to him. What he dreamed of. This sudden insight into his yearning moved me. He was on the inside looking out.

I met another man just getting ready to join a small group in a house in an ordinary residential area outside. He was excited.

A few days later, the hospital manager phoned me. The photos were good, I was told, and then, "You remember __, the man waiting to go out? Well, I met him on the corridor this morning, and asked him how he was. He didn't say anything. He just pulled a Yale key out of his pocket, and smiled. "This is mine now," he said.

He'd found a new freedom and joy. It came with responsibilities too, in an outside world that could be very demanding. But the freedom and joy made the responsibility worthwhile.

It does for us too. Real freedom lies in Jesus Christ. In him we find space we've never known before. And with it comes the demand that we live for him, and share in his work of reconciliation.

Sometimes, Lord, I feel a little caged.
Hemmed in.
My diary's full, the day's agenda fixed.
And when I look ahead it's just the same.
I move from one place to the next
on someone else's timetable.
I'm just a train,
running on fixed lines,
controlled by signals other people make.
I'm started, stopped, and shunted,
by elements outside my grasp.
And all the time
I drag around more baggage than I need.

Exaggerating, Lord?
Maybe I am,
but that's the way it feels.
And yet I'm free to choose
to love and serve.
Or not.
And when I use that freedom,
without thought,
the way I usually do,
I often tread on people's toes.

Lord, in my freedom
give me the love
that steps lightly
on others' sensitivity.
The love that sees my neighbour's life
as holy ground,
not to be trampled on.
Make me aware of other people's hopes.
Make me value their dreams,
give them the space they need
to breathe.

And, Lord,
in all my talk of freedom,
help me remember where it starts.
With you.
That freedom lies in serving you.
That only as I face the truth
about myself
and take your yoke
Will I be free to be myself.

Luke 19:28-38

JESUS came to Jerusalem. The people accepted him with enthusiasm as he rode in, but they missed the significance of his coming. He came as a king, but he came as king on a donkey.

Riding the donkey, he rejected both the reality and the trappings of power. This king-on-a-donkey refused to conform to the expected image, the accepted values of the society of his time. He came humbly, choosing the way of peace. Relying on the quiet persistence of love, rather than the sterile forces of compulsion.

Jesus was a nonconformist, a rebel. Not for the sake of rebellion, and not deliberately. His values were so different from those of his day that they brought him inevitably into conflict.

That's where it all turned sour. It was one thing to challenge the authorities. That's always popular with the people. We enjoy seeing the rich and famous embarrassed. It's comforting to see they don't always get their own way. We applaud as we read of him overturning the tables of the moneychangers, but his lifestyle challenges everyone. Then and now. You and me. Challenges *us* to change, not just the man or woman across the street.

If Jesus entered my city today I've a feeling he'd appear, not in a company car, but on a tatty bicycle, with his trousers tucked into the tops of his socks. And the first call he'd make wouldn't be at the cathedral but at the Job Centre to see who needed help.

I wonder then who'd cry "Hosanna" and who "Crucify"?

Lord, the donkey must have been surprised.
It wasn't used to all that noise.
It wasn't used to people riding on its back.
The flash of clothes
thrown down before its feet
was disconcerting.
Palm branches waving near its eyes,
off-putting.
The shouting of the crowd
incomprehensible.

And yet it seemed content to carry you.
I've seen no record of it rearing up,
or kicking.
It didn't seem to shy,
or back away.
Just plodded on,
the weight of God
light on its back.

I'm not like that.

I'll join the crowd,
cry blessings on you, Lord.
But, then, like them,
my welcome is conditional.
I like the thought
of your disturbing
other people's lives.
I'm with you, Lord,
in pointing out their faults,
and making your demands on them.
It's when you look at me
that I begin to get uncomfortable.

For, suddenly,
you take the tables of my life
and tip them upside down.
And all the things I hold so dear
go rolling down the aisles
of my hypocrisy.
Scattered and lost,
shown up for what they are,
or aren't.
And I stand there before you, empty.

All I can ask, Lord,
is that you'll put into my life
the same humility and willingness
the donkey had.
That bearing you
will be no heavy weight,
your burden light,
your yoke an easy fit.

Cumbrian Cottage

Ephesians 2:1-10

I T was a bitterly cold day. The stems of long grass were etched pale gold against the dark browns and purples of the bare trees. I'd been sketching down by the river, until my fingers were too cold to hold a pencil. I watched an angler packing up. He'd been there four hours, he said, sitting among the reeds, huddled against the wind.

Stowing his rods and other gear away, the last thing he did was take his net out of the river, the net in which he held the fish he'd caught. As he lifted it clear of the water, it almost exploded with energy. There must have been a dozen fish in it, several a respectable size.

He looked at them with quiet satisfaction for a few seconds, then gently released them into the water, giving them their freedom.

As a parable, the story isn't accurate in all its details — parables are often like that — but it made me think of Paul's words to the Christians at Ephesus. "By grace you are saved," he said. When they were caught up in never-ending tangles of selfishness, thrashing around without purpose or hope, God gave them a way out.

He opened the net, restored them to the freedom he'd created them for, but which they'd lost. He gave them freely, graciously, what they had no power to achieve for themselves.

When Jesus called Peter and Andrew to follow him, he told them, "I'll make you fishers of men". In a way, that's almost an image of captivity but, down by the river, I saw it in a new light. We're caught in his net, not to be confined, but to be released to a freedom we could never earn. It's God's gift of grace, free and undeserved.

Lord, I know the feeling.
Netted, like a fish.
Caught up in the pressures
that surround me every day.
I thrash around, gasping for air,
fighting for space,
the urgency allowing no concern for others.
Each struggle weakens me a little more.
Each movement encroaches
on another's freedom.
The net of my own egotism —
and others' expectations —
holds me prisoner.
The mesh restricts me.
And the harder I push
the more it hurts.
I see no way out.

Then comes release.
Your hand reaches down.
Lifts me.
Breathes new life.
Offers new freedom.

And as the mesh falls away
I see the struggle was of my own making.
And poorly made at that.
A do-it-yourself job, if ever there was one.
But this new freedom is yours.
Purpose-made by a craftsman.

And it's a gift.
I get weary of all the promises
that drop through my letterbox.
Glossy, but empty.
New life by mail order,
allow 28 days for delivery.
Yet, somehow, the prize they say I've won already
never comes.

Yours, Lord, unlike the others,
is a gift of grace.
No catch,
the small print honest and to the point.

And in the freedom of your love
I swim with confidence.

John 19:38-42

JOSEPH of Arimathea and Nicodemus are interesting characters. They were twilight disciples — we are told that Nicodemus "first came to Jesus by night". They believed, but stayed in the background during Jesus' lifetime.

Yet when all the others had run away, Joseph and Nicodemus came out into the open. They went to Pilate, and committed themselves openly by asking for Jesus' body.

What intrigues me is the moment they chose to reveal themselves. It seems to be the worst possible time. It was after Jesus had died, and it was before the resurrection.

Somehow, the crisis of the crucifixion gave them the courage to declare where they stood. There was no buoyant hope to carry them along. Jesus was dead, and that seemed to be the end of it. We know that the resurrection lay ahead, but they didn't.

And this was the point at which they went to Pilate. We don't know what went on in their minds, but it suggests to me that the time when faith and action are most important is when things are at their worst. It's not the time to hide and tremble, but the time to do something.

The other thing that strikes me is that at this time of disappointment and danger, the "secret" disciples were the only ones who did show up. All the others were in hiding. And realising that, I wonder if maybe it's time we stopped judging the soundness of our fellow Christians, and the worthiness of their actions, and left that to God. Because we just don't have enough information to do it.

Lord, I wonder where I'd be?
Out in the open,
committing myself publicly,
or cowering in an upper room somewhere?
I think I know.

It's hard being honest,
especially with myself.
Words of commitment come comfortably,
sweetening the day with cut-price sincerity.
Promises.
Buy now, pay later.
Peter did.
I hear him.
"Lord, whatever the rest may do,
I'll never leave you."
That's what he said.
And you and I know what he did.

It makes you think.
Makes me think, anyway.
The easy words,
sincerely meant —
give credit where it's due —
but sparse in understanding.
Easy to say,
when you don't know where they'll lead.
But when the crisis comes,
and promises come home to roost,
then words are not enough.
And with the roosting
comes the sound of cockcrow.

Forgive me, Lord,
I knew not what I said.

Yet failure isn't final.
The quiet ones came out at last.
Out of the shadows.
Found courage in their grief.
Found strength to stand.
To them the blessing
of receiving Christ,
dead, but alive.
Finished, yet just begun.
To them the privilege
of acting host to resurrection.

Lord, help me keep control
of what I say.
And when I don't,
and promise far too much,
and fail,
remember Peter.
And remember me.
And help me start again.

Nottinghamshire Coal Mine

Mark 10:17-23

Y OU might think Jesus was being a bit hard on the young man. He came asking about the way to eternal life. A good motive. And he was trying hard. "I've kept the commandments since I was a boy," he said.

I imagine Jesus with a hint of a smile on his face at this point, listening to the young man's over-confidence. There was, perhaps, just a little self-righteousness in him. None of us is really that good about meeting the demands those commandments make. But Jesus looked at him and loved him.

A strange way he has of showing it though. No congratulations for the way the boy had lived so far, just an uncompromising demand for a complete revolution in his life. "Go, sell . . . give . . . and follow me."

Jesus always stretches us. We move one step forward on the road to life, and he asks another. We show signs of progress, and he shows us there's more to come.

Sometimes, when we love people, we make allowances, give them the easy option, try to smooth the path. Not so Jesus. He's never content with the *status quo*. He's never satisfied with where we're at. He's always encouraging us to grow. Stretching us to our limit, demanding that little bit more.

And, when you think about it, it's a sign of the depth of his love that he makes us reach out for more. A sign of his faith in us, that he believes we're capable of more.

In love, he asks everything from us. He has the right to. That's what he gave.

Lord, sometimes I'd like a breather.
Time off for good behaviour.
Although there's not so much of that about
in my life, I must admit.
Time to relax, admire the view.
And tell myself how well I've done.
Feels like I'm always climbing.

The path is rocky,
narrow, steep.
Heart hammering, blood pumping,
I reach the top
of every small achievement,
look up,
and see the summit's still ahead.
Painfully high.
Stark in still air,
or soft-edged and insubstantial
in tomorrow's mist.
There's always more.

Resentment isn't far away.
Without much effort I could feel hurt.
I'm trying, Lord,
but each hill climbed —
and they're not many, I confess —
leads to another.

And yet where would I be
if love let go?
Left me,
self-satisfied and smug?
If you were as easily content
as I can be
with minuscule achievement?

Thank God,
thank you, you're not.
For each step up I make,
you ask another.
Love says move on.
Stay taut. Stretch tight.
Reach out.
And as I do,
love meets me.
Not standing on the summit,
high and unobtainable until the last,
but climbing with me.

Psalm 23

P SALM 23 is reassuring. The image of the shepherd guiding, guarding and feeding his flock is comforting. Reading it for the umpteenth time the other day, though, something struck me that I'd never noticed before.

The psalmist writes confidently that God guides him in the paths of righteousness, but follows this immediately with "Even though I walk through the valley of the shadow of death. . .".

Leading me in paths of righteousness sounds great, particularly after the green pastures and still waters bit. But then comes the valley of the shadow. . . .

The writer, I assume, saw no contradiction between the two. He's saying that paths of righteousness don't always lead to still waters. And having the right religious passport doesn't guarantee trouble-free travel.

It's echoed in verse five. "You prepare a table for me . . ." but I'm warned that it may be in the presence of my enemies. That "table" isn't a quiet picnic by the lake, when the only discordant note is the ants on the cake. God provides my needs, but it may well be in preparation for the next part of the struggle. My enemies, says the psalmist, are nearby.

But so is the shepherd; not to make life easy, but to surround me with love, and to give me the strength for the next step forward.

Lord, there's always a catch.
I get hooked on the green pastures
and still waters.
I could spend my time very nicely
lying in summer grass.
Content.

And if I felt really energetic
I'd open my eyes
and watch the clouds sail by,
safely, far overhead.
That's where clouds should be.

But when those clouds
draw thick chill curtains over the sun,
their shadows racing over the ground,
I shiver.
And when they come down to ground level,
my level,
shrouding me in mist,
I walk a panic path of fear.
The still surface of my peace shattered.
Rough rippled
by the first breath of wind over the water.

Are these the paths of righteousness?
I pick my way through,
hesitating at every step.
Worried that when I move
my foot may slip, my ankle twist.
And, sometimes, putting out my hand,
there's nothing there.
Or so it seems.

And yet, somehow a strength is there.
Supporting me.

The shepherd takes me high to pasture,
over rocky paths.
Calling me to effort.
I climb,
struggling through thorn thickets,
the way marked by scraps of wool
torn from the fleece of my self-satisfaction.
It makes me breathless.
But you are there.

Counting the sheep.
Knowing when I stray.
Giving your life to rescue me.
Taking me, each day,
nearer the fold.

Towards the Meadow

Matthew 12:46-50

I'VE always found this a difficult story. Jesus lived and taught love. Yet here he is, apparently rejecting the parents who'd cared for him, and who, in human terms, had taught him what love was. Surely he'd had a happy childhood home, or he wouldn't have found love so central to his life, nor talked to God as *Abba*, "Daddy".

Yet here he seems to turn his back on them, and in a hurtful way. I wonder why? Some suggest that family influence tried to hold him back, and that it had to be cut to free him for his work. Maybe so.

I see another element in it. Jesus was Jewish. Jews were born into a ready-made, easily identifiable community. They all shared a religion, a culture and a language. They didn't have to choose it; it was their life.

But Jesus' teaching made choices necessary. Those who chose his way would be rejected by their community, because the community thought of them as rejecting the values that everyone else lived by.

They would have to find a new community, new friends, new family. Not because they wanted to, but because they had no other option. And I believe that when Jesus spoke these words, he wasn't so much rejecting his natural parents, as warning his followers of the things they would have to face. Pointing them to the new family of believers of which they would be a part, and from which they would get their strength and support.

It's just as true today. Whenever people re-orientate their lives in Christ, the old community looks askance. It's more extreme in some cultures than others but it always happens. We need to be prepared for it. And believers need the support of others who believe as they do. Which is why it's so important for the church to be a caring community, governed not so much by rules as by love.

Lord, it can be hard, following you.
Sometimes,
I wonder if you really understand
what it's like being me.

The tensions I live with.
The pressures that build up.
Blowing me all ways at once.
Making me want to scream
like a safety valve letting off steam.

I don't want to be different.
I'd much rather run with the herd.
Be part of the crowd.
Unnoticed. Accepted.
Sticking out like a sore thumb is dangerous.
It gets hurt.
Snagged on the barbs of conformity.

But it happened to you.
I forget that, in my self-pity.

And I can almost hear you echoing my words.
Saying to me
"I wonder if you really understand
what it's like being me".

Forgive me, Lord.
I've got it the wrong way round again.
If anyone found it tough, you did.
If anyone was rejected, you were.
And as for standing out in the crowd —
you got more than a sore thumb.
On the cross.

And that was for me.
And for your mother and family.
What seemed like rejecting them
was just one step
in the painful progress to the cross.
And beyond.
One step in which rejection was rejected,
one step through which we're all
drawn to you in love.

A new community in you.
Open to all.
Mothers, fathers, children.
Me.

John 15:1-10

PRUNING always worries me. I was doing a bit this morning. It seems such a violent, traumatic process. Take a living shoot in one hand, pruning shears in the other, and cut. It's an amputation. It often has to be done drastically, cutting out a whole shoot from one plant, or reducing the whole plant to a fraction of its height. And when you've finished, the plant looks injured.

But wait a bit. Sun, rain, and time bring their reward. Where a single, scarred stem remained, two are shooting out. Or the whole plant is a better shape, gives more blossom, or makes a thicker hedge.

Nature is forgiving. It has the energy, the inner compulsion and ability, to heal the cut. Moving to another area of the living world, the poet William Blake suggests that "the cut worm forgives the plough". What seems an end is a beginning. New life springs from the wounds. Fruit is more plentiful after the pruning.

It would be easy to be glib, and say that suffering is a pruning, and that the pain is worthwhile because of its fruits. I can't go that far. Suffering's a mystery to me. And if it isn't to you then maybe you don't understand that you don't understand. Suffering *can* work wonders, strengthen character, bring fruit; but it doesn't always. It can damage and break, too. It can cripple emotionally as well as physically.

Perhaps the clue is in our being branches of the vine, which is Christ. Secure in him, the pruning is positive. It still hurts, we still feel like screaming, but we know he's there, and that he's gone through the same process himself. Maybe we need to remember that the cross began as a tree.

Lord, the pious words
of righteous people
don't always ring a bell with me.
Faced with the pain of suffering,
disappointment, damaged hopes,
whether it's my pain or another's,
I find it hard to hear it said
that God knows best.

I know you do,
but to load responsibility on you,
to imply that, somehow,
that makes it right and proper
that people suffer,
isn't a satisfying answer.

And when, sometimes,
I shout to you out loud,
the answer that I get
is deafening silence.
That's not so helpful either.
Then, I'm thrown back upon myself,
and see my own vulnerability.
And out of that grows prayer.
Because it's only out of need
that real prayer comes.
Or so it seems.

The cut worm, the pruned branch,
both bleed, each in its own way.
And in the bleeding lies its healing.
Lies new growth.
One of the many miracles of daily life.

Lord, when I scream,
and others too,
gather us to yourself.
Help me to see, and them,
that understanding isn't all that matters.
Isn't at the root of things.
The truth is,
that when I'm grafted into you,
my pain is your pain.
My groan your groan.
And your healing is mine.
In time.
And in eternity.

Hebrews 12:1-2

A PROMINENT Christian was suffering from terminal cancer. He was interviewed on radio a week before his death — not that he knew that at the time. He was asked about his faith. He said that, as time went on, he believed "more and more about less and less".

It struck a chord. It seems to me that as faith grows it becomes possible to let go many of the things we once thought important, in order to hold more strongly to the few things that do matter.

Another cancer sufferer, a woman, said that being brought face to face with serious illness had made her jettison the trivia of her life to concentrate on the few really important things.

Neither of them said what those truly important things were. It's tempting to try to define them, to make assumptions, but that wouldn't be honest. They may be different for different people. What may have been important to one, may not have been so for the other.

The point to grasp is that life is often cluttered, and the clamour of the trivial can overlay the things that are essential. Our attention is so easily diverted. There is a modesty about the important — it frequently stands back and waits for us to notice, knowing that its time will come.

Knowing that sooner or later we have to come back to basic values. To decide what's important for us as individuals, and let the rest go.

Lord, there's something in my nature
that takes me, so easily,
like moth to light,
to things that don't matter.
I circle and flutter,
batter wings,
fly frantic for nothing.

I fill my time with trivia.
Crowd out the questions
of who I really am,
and where I'm heading.
In a panic progress
I persuade myself
— at least I try to —
that here and now is my concern.
Then I discover
that the yellow brick road
of my own feelings
leads,
not to fulfilment,
but circles back to starting point.
And I'm left
holding an A to Z of Nowhere.

Lord, calm me down.
Inject a moment's peace
into the bloodstream of my life.
And in the peace
help me to see the world whole.
Or, if that's too much to ask,
at least to see myself
for what I am.

Give me the courage
to dive below the surface,
to push aside the jetsam of my living,
to catch a vision of what really matters,
not in a kaleidoscope of jumbled images,
changing with every twist of the tube,
but clear and fresh
in the light of your truth.
Help me to grasp priorities,
to understand a little
of your purpose for the world,
and my place in it.

Help me to differentiate
the urgent from the important.
To hear, behind the clamorous voice of now,
your gentle voice that offers me,
so quietly,
the joy of knowing why I'm here,
and who stands close.

Lake District Farm House

1 Corinthians 13

WHEN we moved house recently, we had to find a new plumber. It wasn't easy getting one, but when Jim turned up he was very helpful. He's a competent, conscientious and cheerful worker, and a conversationalist.

He told us a lot about his family. There's a teenage son, tragically hit by multiple sclerosis, and a wife Jim obviously adores. "She's a great woman, my wife," he said, "and we've got a good marriage. In 30 years she's never run out of coffee or toilet paper." We laughed.

There are many ways of showing love. The glossy magazines say diamonds are best. The slightly more modest weeklies advise us to say it with flowers. A hug, a kiss, a held hand, all help.

And there's the coffee and toilet paper way. The faithful, quiet work that keeps homes going, keeps relationships good. The attention to detail, making sure that the everyday things are cared for. It may be earthy, but it's no less valuable for that.

The cup of coffee, and the rest, speak for themselves. Speak of looking ahead, anticipating needs, meeting them with loving ordinariness.

"Love is patient; love is kind . . .", writes Paul to Christians at Corinth, "Love will never come to an end". And whether we write books about it, or express it simply through the weekly shopping list, it all has meaning. Love expressed in an infinity of ways, mostly quiet.

Love is still at the centre of the universe. Still available. And God, who is love, is still trying to pour it into our lives.

So many ways, Lord,
in which you show your love.
Sometimes, its very ordinariness
surprises me.
No drama here,
no lightning flash or thunder-clap.
Just faithfulness,
in spite of all I do
to make it difficult.
I make myself unlovely,
yet still your love surrounds me,
seeks out the cracks
in the hard shell of my ego,
and seeps in unrecognised.

I think I could identify a miracle,
but the unassuming wonder
of your daily love
I take for granted,
fail to see.
Lord, out of that same love,
forgive me.

And help me realise
the many ways
in which I can transmute your love
within the daily chemistry of my life.
Help me to show I care,
by word, by touch,
by the warmth of shared thought.
By simple service, anticipating need.
Samaritan compassion on the road.
A hand reached out
to stem another's hurt.
A cup of water on the way
to crucifixion.

And that reminds me, Lord,
that what I do
for any traveller on the road,
I do for you.
That any love I share
I share with you,
and you with me.
Please help me keep that
in the forefront of my mind,
today.

Luke 12:6-7

AND the kingdom of heaven is like this: we asked a local carpenter to put in two new wooden gateposts. He said he'd buy them, soak them in creosote to preserve them, and then come and do the job.

We waited. Nothing happened. Then he phoned. "Sorry for the delay," he said. "I soaked the posts and put them in the back of my workshop to dry. When I went to get them I found a pair of blackbirds had made a nest on them, and now there's a brood of fledgelings there. I haven't the heart to disturb them. I'll come when they've flown."

We agreed, happily.

It's a little thing, and blackbirds are one of the most common of British birds. But how reassuring to find a man with values like that. Our culture is so profit-orientated, so geared to money, that nothing else seems to matter.

Here, in a small way, is someone saying that life matters, however small the dividend seems. There are other values besides gain, values which bring richness to life, richness beyond riches.

Incidentally, when the birds had flown and he came to do the work, he brought the nest to show us. The marks of the posts were clear to see. Just a family of small, common birds, but I think Jesus would have made a parable out of the story.

All it needed, Lord,
was a little time.
A bit of patience.
A few more days.
But it would have been so easy
to disturb the nest.
"I need the wood for a gate,"
he could have said.
"What's all the fuss about?"
And trampled on the future.

It's so easy to ignore
the little things.
Things with no voice,
no influence.
No strings to pull.
The small and insignificant.
And yet, Lord,
saying that
is judgement I've no right to make.
Small and insignificant to whom?
No sparrow falls, you said,
without God knowing.
You, like the carpenter,
concerned for little things.
You, as a carpenter,
caring that the least
should find a place of value
in your kingdom.
A kingdom for the poor and weak.

If influence found favour
in your sight,
if privilege bought places
in your kingdom,
there'd be
a lot of empty places there.
And when I look at me,
I'm glad your kingdom takes
the weak and struggling.
For that gives me a chance.
I stand renewed in hope.
Stand confident,
not in the righteousness
I sometimes kid myself about —
just puffed up feathers

on a frosty morning —
but in your wide compassion.

And in response, Lord,
give me a ready understanding,
for all who have no power.
Give me the carpenter's sympathy
and love for little things.
Help me find value in the undervalued,
find worth in things
without a price tag.

I like to think the carpenter,
one day,
may share a glance with you, Lord,
one carpenter to another,
because he shared
your love of little things.
And if the gateposts of your kingdom
should ever need repairing,
perhaps you'll think of him.

Misty Morning Walk

Mark 15:33-39

THREE gospel writers each tell us about the veil of the temple being torn in two as Jesus died on the cross. It was important to them.

The temple in Jerusalem wasn't just a place for sacrifice and worship. To the Jewish people, it was the place where the Spirit of God lived on earth. The central part of the temple was the Holy of Holies, and God was there. It had no door, but was screened from the rest of the temple by a heavy curtain — the veil.

No-one but the high priest could enter, and he only once a year, at Yom Kippur, the Day of Atonement.

Bible commentators catch hold of the symbolism of the torn curtain. In Jesus' death, they say, the way to God is thrown open, and men and women can approach him freely in a new relationship.

I see another angle to it. The tearing of the curtain not only lets us in, it lets the Spirit of God out. God can't be contained.

Holiness is no longer boxed in, but released into the world. Through the cross, it pours out in a flood to swamp us — not in dread and guilt, but in love and wonder.

Lord, I'm swimming
in the wonder of it all.
That in your love,
and through your suffering,
the obstacles
that stand between us
are torn apart.

At your initiative
the sea wall is breached,
the floodgates opened wide,
your Spirit loosed upon the world.
And, sink or swim,
I'm caught up in a tide of hope,
held on the flood.

I grasp the wonder,
but I must confess
the times it's frightened me.
Still does,
this flood of holiness.
I'd rather paddle gently
in the shallows,
than strike out into your depths.
Put out a toe, cautious thermometer,
to feel the cold
before I take the plunge.
Your sea is wider than my imagination,
your waves higher than my courage.

Its gentleness can be deceptive.
There are times when I can feel its winds,
storm force, blow through my life
with strength that leaves me breathless.
Uncomfortable, Lord.

And then I am reminded
that the storms, the calms,
are in your hands.

You stilled the sea.
Still me.

1 Corinthians 1:26-31

THE other Sunday we worshipped in a little Methodist church in a Midlands country town. The minister was away, preaching at another of the communities in his care.

His place was taken by an old man. He'd been over six feet tall, but now was bent like an old tree. He walked awkwardly, pulling himself up the stairs to the pulpit with difficulty. He had a heavy face, big brows, prominent cheekbones. His hands were enormous, gnarled and worn. I don't know, but I guess he'd been either a farm worker or a miner. He'd a strong local accent which obviously had no time to waste on aitches.

I don't think he'd ever been taught to preach, or how to present himself, but he obviously enjoyed sharing his faith and experience with others. He valued words, and didn't waste any.

He talked quietly, intimately, and with bright flashes of dry humour which lightened his serious looks. He knew the Bible thoroughly, in the authorised version of course — Good News Bibles and other modern translations weren't for him. He prayed in *thees* and *thous*. There was, as we say in these parts, "no side to him". There was no pretence; he was real. Totally genuine; rough, but 24 carat.

Sitting there I thought maybe this is what some of the first disciples were like, the men Jesus called. Without much formal education, and with no sophistication — which is really only veneer, when you think about it. Just honest, straightforward people, and Jesus changed the world through them.

And he goes on doing it through just such people. St Paul reminds us that not many of us are wise or influential. But God chose the foolish to shame the wise. Chose, and chooses, weak people to shame the strong. Our wisdom's in Christ, and it's not ours, but God's.

And his wisdom clothes us with a dignity that many can't see, but which is there nevertheless. A dignity that doesn't depend on accent or formal education, but springs unbidden out of devotion. Something to treasure when we see it, something to rejoice in, and thank God for.

Lord, I find it hard to understand,
your emphasis on weak and foolish.
The world just laughs,
and turns its back.
The testing ground
is marketplace and jungle.
The tough survive
in the killing fields of commerce.
The weak to the wall.
Their epitaphs written in bank balances.
Black or red.

Not very different in your day.
I see you
surrounded by the strong.
Romans, armoured in authority.
Priests, implacable in piety.
Manipulating the gold of betrayal
and taking a profit.
Making a killing, as we say.

Yet when you look beyond the obvious,
the show of strength is flawed.
Vulnerable.
Strength made brittle
by a core of fear.
Hollow men,
their anguish echoing deep within.

I turn to you.
And here I see
no show of strength,
coercing me to faith.
Rather a quiet patience,
loving me to surrender.
Your weakness strengthened
by a core of love,
resilient as life.
Springing renewed from every pruning.
Surviving, growing,
its annual returns
measured in mercy.

Lord, if it's the weak you want,
the foolish,
then I'm the one.

Well-qualified in weakness,
postgraduate in foolishness.
No other qualities but those.
And a glimmer of faith —
weak like the rest —
for you to use.
You'll need a miracle a day
to keep me going.
But if anyone can do it, Lord,
you can.

South Indian Beach

Matthew 5:9

EIGHTEEN years ago the Kirov Ballet came to London from the USSR. One of their leading ballerinas, Natalia Makarova, defected to the West, "for artistic freedom". Great bitterness and many accusations followed.

Recently, the Kirov returned to London to dance again. With all the political changes in the Soviet Union, and the new spirit of openness, they invited Natalia Makarova to dance with them.

It was an emotional reunion. She danced the classical *pas de deux* from Swan Lake. I can't judge the finer points of the dance, but others who know said it was superb. To me the beauty of the performance was intensified by the beauty of the reconciliation. The bitterness had been put aside. Maybe only after a struggle, but it was gone. Perhaps differences of philosophy and understanding remained, but there was a new spirit at work.

The two dancers on stage were working out a new relationship in trust — surely there can be no dance at this level of artistry without it. Even an amateur like me can see that.

They were dancing out forgiveness. I remembered Sidney Carter's song *Lord of the dance.* Jesus, Lord of the dance of life, draws men and women together across the divisions of a fallen world. And we saw it happening in the Kirov Ballet. Unwittingly, perhaps, but true nonetheless and, with a beauty that surpassed the ballet, we saw the beauty of reconciliation.

Lord, I don't know how it is,
but we've turned
the beauty of the world you made
into a desert.
Cut down the forests of your love
with sharpened blades of hate.
Polluted the rivers of your grace
with selfishness.
We've brought division,
built barriers,
marked boundaries.
And from the steps and platforms
of our dogmas,
shouted war.
We've found it easy to destroy,
by indifference as much as evil.
We're learning now
how hard it is
to build and re-create.

And yet you love us.
Can love be so elastic
that it stretches out and out
to take in all we've done
and still forgive?
You tell us so.
And show it in torn hands,
marked hard by crucifixion.

Lord, stand with us at the barricades.
And help us, not to fight,
but to dismantle them.
Help us to open up
the road to reconciliation.
To plant and water seeds of trust.
To reach out hands of love,
take partners,
dance forgiveness.

Genesis 4:3-9

THE other day, my wife Barbara took the car to Richmond Park, on the outskirts of London. When she got back we noticed that the car was covered in a fine, brown dust. The past few days had been warm and dry so we thought no more about it, except to wash the car down.

Next day, a commentator reported on the radio that freak winds and weather conditions had brought dust from North Africa, and that the fine film many people had noticed on their cars in London had come from the Sahara.

So far away, yet so near. What's in the Sahara Desert one day can end up on my car the next. We all share the same world, and what happens in one part of it can affect what happens elsewhere. Sometimes, it's more important than dust on cars. The nuclear accident in Chernobyl, in the Soviet Union, poisoned sheep pastures in Britain. Acid waste from UK factories kills trees in Scandinavia.

We don't live to ourselves. What we do affects our neighbours, often more than we realise. When God asked Cain about his brother Abel, Cain tried to shrug off all responsibility. "Am I my brother's keeper?" he asked. The answer, even then, was an uncomfortable "Yes, you are".

And that goes for today, as well. We can't live in a tight little circle of comfort and belief, looking inward, pretending that nothing else exists or matters. There are other people out there, important issues, each demanding a response from us. Being Christian isn't a let-out. It doesn't allow us to spiritualise it all, to withdraw into prayer circles and leave the world to others. It's our world, a shared responsibility. We're one with the rest of humanity, one before God. Whether we like it or not we are our brother's keeper, and there's no way we can shuffle out of it.

Lord, it would be nice
if it could be just you and me,
in a tight little circle of love.
Holding hands, doors closed.
Drawing the curtains of my mind
on the storm outside.
Blotting the world out.

I remember as a child
sitting under the table
covered in a borrowed sheet.
My fantasy world,
complete with roof and walls.
Hidden from reality.
Inviolate.
Do not disturb.
Not even the cat.

I'd like that, Lord.
We'd be magnanimous —
at times we'd graciously invite
people of like mind
to share our room.
Sympathetic people,
minds small as mine.

The trouble is my world's grown up,
faster than I have.
I can't control it any more.
however much I stuff the rabbit
back into the hat,
it doesn't disappear.

People shout loud.
The sound they make
penetrates the double glazing
of my preoccupations.
No matter where I turn,
which way I face,
however much I block my ears
with selfishness,
the sound gets through.
Disturbs me.

I turn back to you for reassurance,
and find you gone.

The chair you sat in
cold and empty.
I look outside,
lifting the curtain just enough,
and see you in the crowd.
Among the ones I find it hard to face.

I see your hand
beckoning me out.
I hear your voice
telling me
that that's where you belong.
And saying clearly,
that if I'm really yours,
that's where I should be too.
If not to enjoy the fun,
at least to share with you
the dangers and excitement of the road.
To join the dance.

Feeding the Geese

Romans 6:1-4

I'VE been painting for years now, and I know something about water-colour, particularly. A couple of days ago, a free sample came through the post. It was just a small pan of a colour I'd never used before — an oxide of red. My immediate inclination was to throw it in a drawer along with others I've collected on the way. Why alter one's formulae and methods, well-tried and reliable?

But the colour came from a well-known manufacturer who guaranteed its quality, so I thought I'd try it.

It's a lovely colour, a rich red brown, deep and transparent. Used judiciously, it gives a lovely glow to yellows, and contrasts beautifully with deep blues. It's added something new, something worth holding on to, in my colour work.

How often we cling to the comfortable truths we know, and walk well-trodden paths of routine, almost fearful of anything new. At times we show an "if it's new it must be bad" syndrome in our lives. The "I know what I like" attitude so easily becomes "I like what I know", and we confine ourselves in a pen of self-satisfaction. And doing so, we miss the joy of discovery.

Christ calls us to walk a new path, and we can't always see where it leads. Yes, it's risky, and it can be frightening. Living openly calls for both courage and discernment, to risk mistakes and misunderstandings.

But that's how we grow, and we all need to do that.

It scares me, Lord,
the thought of so much change.
At times, I'm petrified,
a hunted creature,
crouched mute in long grass,
the only sound the pulse beat in my head.
And when I get the chance
I run for cover,
hoping I won't be noticed.
Praying that change may pass by
silently on hawk's wings,
its shadow sliding softly out of vision.
And leaving me to breathe again.
Life just as it was.
Uninterrupted, undisturbed.

It doesn't work that way.
Your world, my world,
so solid to the touch,
is constant change.
Growth, and renewal.
And if it weren't,
where would I be?
My only hope is in the change
you've worked in me.
Are working.
Renewing me each day,
and, hopefully,
moulding that quiet transformation
which makes me, slowly,
more like you.

I welcome that.
At least, I do in my best moments.
I see the need,
and though I sometimes feel the pain,
the outcome's sure.
Lord, help me find the courage to adventure,
the willingness to take the risks
that living for you brings.

And let me know the joy
of walking close to you,
my ever-changing,
yet unchanging Lord.

Ephesians 3:8-9

READING a new hymn today, I came across the phrase: "... for the truths that still confound us, thanks be to God".

It's a provocative thought. It's so easy to think that truth is simple, all a matter of black and white. Right or wrong. Sometimes it is, and its stark simplicity challenges us to live in its light. But at other times it's much more complicated, and life's a puzzling mixture of light and shade, and dimly-seen paths.

As I write, two news items conflict. In one, the Episcopal Church in America has elected its first woman bishop. In the other, the Pope has pronounced, with great certainty, that women priests are contrary to the will of Jesus Christ. They can't both be right.

Whatever the truth is, let's acknowledge the anguish conflict causes, and let's recognise too the sincerity of those involved — even if we're tempted at times to say "blind sincerity". Both groups seek earnestly for truth. Both believe they've found it. Both believe they're within God's will.

In most matters, truth, so simple for some to see, becomes a complex issue for others. Some Christians deal in simple certainties. For others, faith involves the courage to hang on when life is complex and problematical.

I take comfort from two thoughts. The first is from George Braque, the painter who shares the credit for Cubism with Picasso. He said, "Truth exists, only falsehood has to be invented". It's there alright, waiting for us.

The second encouragement comes from St Paul, who tells the Christians in Ephesus about "... the unsearchable riches of Christ ...".

Other translations use words like "unfathomable", "infinite". How can we finite people grasp the infinite? How can we, the created, capture the creator? How can we, with our superficial understanding, measure the depths of God's truth? However far or deep we go, there's always more.

We live by what we know. We try to stay faithful to what we believe. But we need to accept that we see darkly, and that the whole of God's glorious light waits for us further on. So, with the hymnwriter, I thank God for truths that still confound me, and rejoice that I can never exhaust his riches. There's always more to come, when I'm ready to take it.

Lord, there are moments
when I'm honest enough to admit
I'm not infallible.
Not often, Lord.
Just now and then,
I'm able to acknowledge
a few small areas of life
where I'm not completely in control.
I admit at times
that life bewilders me
with grey half-tones,
when I'd like to see it all
in black and white.
Retreat for comfort
into simple certainties.
The trouble is, Lord,
that my certainties conflict
with other people's certainties.
And that confuses me.
Makes judgement harder.

Yet through the uncertainties,
I sense your hand,
pushing me into deeper water.
Not so that I risk drowning,
although it sometimes feels that way,
but so that I may swim more strongly.
Learn to think and feel
with greater sensitivity.

So, Lord, where certainties collide,
give me the openness to look afresh,
not only at what others think,
but at my own beliefs.
And when the tension shows,
and understanding goes away on holiday,
help me to love.
And wait for you,
Spirit of truth,
to lead me deeper into truth.
Whatever it may be.

John 21:20-22

THE Russian Orthodox Church has just celebrated 1,000 years of life and witness. A recent television programme showed a service of thanksgiving in Moscow Cathedral. The Byzantine splendour of its ritual was moving. Priests in rich robes and hats, icons with an air of mystery beyond art, choirs singing velvet harmonies that seemed to draw beauty out of the stones themselves.

The worshippers were very mixed in appearance, but one in devotion. There were traditional *babushkas* — old women in shawls — but there were others too — young men and women, peasants and more sophisticated town dwellers. All rejoicing in the new freedom which political *glasnost* has brought to the Church.

An interviewer asked a priest about the hard times of persecution. Part of his answer stuck in my mind. "The old went more daringly to church," he said, "But the young kept prayer alive in their hearts". Who, I wondered, showed the greater devotion? Those who took risks openly by going to public worship? Or those who quietly but faithfully lived inner lives of prayer and patience?

I don't know. We Christians are sometimes too glib and superficial in our judgements. The questions in my mind are answered only by another question, "Who am I to judge?"

"And what about him, Lord?" asked Peter, looking at John. "What is that to you?" replied Jesus, "You follow me". The words imply that when I've got my act together, then I may have a right to ask. When loving comes as naturally to me as it does to Jesus, then my comment may be worth listening to. And laced, perhaps, with a little more understanding.

Lord, one thing I'm good at —
criticising other people.
Self-taught,
I've had a lot of practice.
Probably true to say,
I've made it into an art form.
There's nothing, no-one
I can't see through.
Probing for weakness,
I can find the hidden flaw
that brings the value of anything
crushing down.

And when it comes to labelling
my fellow Christians,
I'm superb.
And quick.
Split-second judgement,
based firmly on my prejudice.
And stamina — I've got enough
to run a marathon of criticism.
It only needs a louder voice,
or longer hair,
a liking for hymns that I don't sing,
and I'm away.
Feeding my derision
with the rich compost of cynicism,
my superiority creating
a thick-leaved canopy
beneath which nothing else can grow.
A thick forest of sterility.

Lord, there's something wrong.
That's obvious, even to me.
It's easy to identify,
but hard to fight.

Teach me to rest in you.
To find my joy and satisfaction,
not in proving to myself
how much above the rest I am,
but in the realisation
that I'm loved.
That you love me without conditions.
And that gives me
a worth beyond imagining.

Lord, if I'm loved like that,
with all the faults
I hesitate even to list,
prefer to ignore,
then maybe, slowly,
I can start to see the good in others.
Discount the differences.
Perhaps begin to see
the richness that they bring to life.
And slowly, find it possible
to love a little.

Edge of the Woods

John 21:1-7

ON Easter morning, Mary finds Jesus' tomb empty, and stands in the garden, weeping for her loss. Jesus comes to her, but she doesn't recognise him immediately. She thinks he's the gardener.

A few days later, Peter and some of the other disciples take a boat and go fishing in Galilee. Jesus calls to them from the shore, but they don't realise at first who he is. Two other disciples, walking the road to Emmaus, meet a stranger. Going with them, he talks, explains and comforts. Again, it's Jesus.

I don't know why these close friends of Jesus didn't recognise him straight away. I don't understand what made him different after the resurrection. It isn't really important that I should.

The important thing is to realise that Jesus is unpredictable. He shows himself in whatever way he chooses. Not capriciously, but in ways that startle, puzzle us, surprise us out of our easy assumptions. Ways that widen our awareness.

In our insecurity, we try to make rules. "This is how Christians should act." "This is how you recognise the Holy Spirit." "This is how...." And hard luck the Christian who breaks our rules. But Jesus breaks them all the time.

He broke the Sabbath rules to heal the sick, to respond to need with love, not law. And he still breaks them, to tell us that life can't be lived in a self-imposed straitjacket, that he can't be contained within our limited vision. That life is an unpredictable adventure, but that he's in it with us, even though we can't always see him, don't always recognise him. He tells us to look for goodness in unlikely places, to find him in unlikely people.

And when we open our closed and timid minds to the glory of his presence, we shall find him everywhere and in everyone.

You ask so much, Lord.
Somehow,
I'm meant to see the invisible.
Discern you in the unexpected.
Allow infinity into my life.
You offer me eternity,
but just the simple,
not so simple, act
of living out today,
demands all I can give.
My little mind asks certainty,
the comfort of particularity.
Of knowing where I am,
and what I'm meant to do.
I seek the refuge of routine,
blinker myself in pettiness.

My mind can't span
the wonder of your love.
My pigmy courage can't accept
the challenge of your presence.
Sometimes I think it's easier
to stand outside your empty tomb
and weep,
than look into your eyes
and see the resurrection.
Lord, let me understand
that caution
kills the joy of knowing you.
That life with you
goes far beyond the safe.
That I must make the leap of faith
into the dark.
But, making it,
my senses come alive.
Emerge,
shake off constriction,
unfold their wings,
and fly.

And, life enriched,
I see your face
in people I have never seen before.
I hear your voice
in ways I couldn't comprehend.

Easter is every day.

Luke 10:29-37

THERE'S a television comedy called "Bread". It centres on a family in Liverpool, mother, father and grown-up children. Grandad lives in the house next door.

In a recent episode, Grandad was unhappy. He felt lonely, and showed it in bad temper when they called round to see him. The family responded by taking him little gifts, to show they loved him.

It didn't satisfy Grandad. "I don't want you to give me things," he complained, "I just want you to stay awhile".

In their busyness, it was hard for the family to realise that he didn't want gifts, he just needed them. A little of their time.

It's a perceptive parable. When someone's in need, it's usually easier to raise a collection for them than to find people with the time to go and be with them.

Love *can* be shown through gifts, but the best gift is often one's time. Love is a relationship, reaching out across the gap between people, pulling them closer. When someone's lonely, it's not *presents* they want, it's *presence*. Someone to sit with, to talk to, someone to listen. Someone who values them enough not just to give their money but to give their time.

The important thing about the Good Samaritan, it seems to me, wasn't the fact that he had money. It was his willingness to give time, take risks, and develop a relationship.

If we're too busy for this, then we're too busy.

Lord, life's a whirlpool.
So much to do.
I rush around, faster and faster,
intent on today,
this moment.
Never looking beyond the immediate.
My good intentions,
wet and waterlogged,
slide down the plug hole.
Gone.

Out there,
on the blurred edge of vision,
people stand, beckon, call.
So indistinct I can pretend
I don't see them,
except to myself.
But I rush on.
No time.
Scattering, perhaps,
a little largesse on the way.
Greasing the palm of charity.
My once bright conscience dulled
with tarnished generosity.
Encrusted rust, self-damaging.
My own collecting boxes
full of good intentions,
never cashed.

And yet, Lord,
there are moments
when I hear your voice.
Soft, yet insistent.
Your voice, coming,
not from some cloudy heaven
above, beyond,
but somehow centred
in the people I ignore.
And when I take my courage in both hands —
and doing that
means putting down my diary first —
and turn to them,
I find I've turned to you.
Among the lonely.
You are the neighbour I ignored.
The injured on the Jericho road.

And when I walk by,
on the other side,
I sidestep love,
and I'm the lonely one.
Self-exiled by my busyness.

Lord, help me try again.
Find time for others.
Find time for you.

Beech Trees.

Matthew 10:26-31

ON holiday in the Lake District we went to the parish church on Sunday morning. As we walked in, we were handed a sheet of notices, along with the hymn book. Sitting in the quiet before the service began, I read through the notices. They were mainly details of the coming week's events, but at the bottom of the page was a short list of items for prayer.

I read them. First came "Pray for world leaders in Geneva, talking about nuclear disarmament". Next, "Pray for Maggie Smith and her housing problem".

I smiled to myself. It seemed a bit incongruous. First, the subject of earth-shattering nuclear weapons, and their control. The tensions between Washington and Moscow, with ourselves in the middle. And, next to it, Maggie Smith and her house. It was important to her, I was sure, but it was a small local problem that would never hit the headlines.

On second thoughts though, it wasn't incongruous at all. That's what God is like. He's concerned about every aspect of life, everyone's life. Yours and mine. God tells the prophet Haggai, "I will shake the nations . . ." (Haggai 2:7). And Jesus assures us, "Not a sparrow will fall to the ground apart from the will of your Father". And that's all the same God.

Nothing too large for him, nothing too small. He's as concerned about my small problems and needs as he is about the great political issues. As concerned about my future as about the world's.

Whatever concerns us today, he's there with us, lovingly involved, and we can take comfort.

A tall order, Lord.
Expecting you to be concerned about the lot.
Nothing too large, nothing too small.
Yet that's exactly what he said.
Jesus, I mean.
"Your heavenly Father knows," he said.

It's reassuring, once my scepticism goes to sleep.
I must admit to lingering doubts at times.
There are bits of me that wonder if it's really true.
Perhaps because there are bits of me
I wish you didn't know or care about.
Parts of my life I'd rather hide away.
Lock up, and throw away the key.

I'm doing it again, Lord.
Making you in my own image.
Fashioning a god I can control,
predict, be comfortable with.
Not worth the effort though.
A god made in my image wouldn't work.

Who wants a god who doesn't care?
Or, just as bad, a god who doesn't know?
What strength or joy can flow from flawed divinity?
If I could gain your love
only by putting on a mask,
pretending other than I am,
there'd be no point.

Your love is love
because you know precisely who I am,
and what I do, yet love me still.
And value me beyond the sparrow fall.

And not just me.
I'm not the centre of your world,
although I think I am at times.
Your love encompasses creation's struggle,
music of planets, cosmic cries.
The pain and heartbreak
of a world in conflict with itself.

Lord of the great,
it's difficult to understand quite how,
but all the world's concerns that scare me so,
are somehow in your hands.
And taking that to heart, I find my courage
a little greater than it was before.

Revelation 21:1-5

NOW in his eighties, the author Laurens van der Post was walking through one of the remaining wild parts of his beloved Africa.

His companion referred gently to his age and asked, "Laurens, are you looking at all this as though it might be the last time you see it?"

"Yes, there's always that thought," he replied, "But it's much more important to try and see it as though for the first time".

Think about it. There's more wonder in it that way. To see something you love, as you did the first time. The joy of discovery, the sudden breathtaking revelation of beauty — whether a view of nature, a painting, a piece of music, or a person.

We grow used to things, to people. We grow comfortable with them. It's a good thing in its own way, a quieter, different kind of love. But that can slip imperceptibly, dangerously, into a taking for granted, into a lack of appreciation.

"Behold," says Jesus, "I make all things new". In him we are given a new view of the world, and of people, a new vision of what creation was meant to be. Something glorious and full of beauty. A world of wonder and delight.

And look at what we've made of it. Forgive us, Lord.

Today's a day like any other, Lord.
Routine to face.
The practised motions
of a well-worn life.
Same garden path as yesterday,
same bus, same train.
I am my own guide dog,
taking myself across the road
and down the steps
like every day.
My mind in neutral,
nearly stalled.

Same people too.
Performing their routine
as I do mine.
Same tired acts,
all wearing out the elbows of their lives.
Without a conscious thought.
And my acceptance of their presence
thoughtless too.

Lord, I was blind
and then I saw,
and now I'm blind again.
The wonder of it all,
the beauty and the joy,
near gone.
The colours dulled to grey,
muddied and blurred.
I take your world for granted,
and your people.

And that's not all.
Your presence on the road
no longer flashes lightning in my way.
Or if it does,
I fail to notice it.
It seeps away,
safe earthed
by my preoccupations.

Restore my vision, Lord.
Give me again
the multicoloured magic of first sight.
The glimpse of glory
in the lives

of those I meet today.
A fresh appreciation
of their worth.

And let me see you too,
with wonder,
as I saw you first.

Venice

2 Corinthians 2:14-16

AN African Christian from Angola was describing the damage war had done to a mission station. The mission bungalow had been destroyed, he said, but the honeysuckle was still there in the garden....

It touched me. The brick and concrete building, built so strongly and with such hope, was now a heap of rubble. The plant, vulnerable and delicate, somehow had survived. And continued to perfume the air.

When the things we humans build are gone, nature continues. Grows and blossoms. Fills the air with scent. Fills the eyes with beauty. Reminds us how persistent life is. And tells us again how patient God is.

It's a parable of hope. Our best efforts and plans may be shattered by violence, as people struggle for power and advantage. Anger explodes, but when the guns have moved on, there in the rubble of pain and anguish, God begins again. Pulls life together. Gives us another chance.

One day, perhaps, we'll take it, and the smell of honeysuckle will push out the smell of fear. Then we shall be whole again, and through us, the fragrance of Christ will spread abroad, intangible but indestructible.

Lord, it's a bit insubstantial,
honeysuckle against explosive.
Love against hate.
Forgiveness against violence.

And yet it's your way.
A way of patience, suffering,
and vulnerability.
It's hard.
I like the theory,
but when it comes to living,
then I reach for something firmer.
I like the strength of walls,
deceptive shelter,
things I can hold,
and count, and see.

But you, Lord,
had nowhere,
no home to lay your head.
No empire,
not even a Barclaycard.
No army.
Just a few men and women,
simple folk,
vulnerable as you.
People like Peter,
whirling like a weathercock in a storm,
facing all ways.
Yet you chose him to be a rock.

And built a kingdom of hope.
Not to be measured by this world.
Intangible as perfume.
Moving like the wind.
Blowing where it will,
over the walls that divide us.
A breeze of hope,
turning the flank of opposition.
Covering the stale smell
of old fears and infidelities
with the fragrance of forgiveness.

Teach us, Lord,
that love can't be measured,
eternity can't be weighed.
Just lived.
And put a little in my heart today.

Index

REPRESENTATIVE OFFICES

Head Office: 80 Windmill Road, Brentford, Middlesex TW8 0QH, UK

Australia: PO Box 293, Box Hill, Victoria 3128
Tel: 61 3 9890 0515 *Fax:* 61 3 9890 0550

Belgium: PO Box 20, 1800 Vilwoorde *Tel/Fax:* 32 22519983

Canada: 40 Wynford Drive, Suite 216, Don Mills, Ontario M3C 1J5
Tel: 1 416 4413618 *Fax:* 1 416 4410203

Denmark: Pile Alle 3, 2000 Frederiksberg
Tel: 45 31 228616 *Fax:* 45 31 237872

England and Wales, The Channel Islands and The Isle of Man: Goldhay Way, Orton Goldhay, Peterborough PE2 5GZ
Tel: (44) 01733 370505 *Fax:* (44) 01733 370960

Finland: PL 160, 00211 Helsinki
Tel: 358 0 692 3690 *Fax:* 358 0 692 4323

France: BP 186, 63204 Riom Cedex *Tel:* 33 73 387660

Germany: Kuferstr. 12, 73728 Esslingen
Tel: 49 711 353072 *Fax:* 49 711 3508412

Hong Kong: 8B1 Waldorf Mansion, 2 Causeway Road, Causeway Bay
Tel: 852 2890 6062 *Fax:* 852 2890 7855

Hungary: Alagi Ter 13, Budapest 1151

India: CNI Bhavan, 16 Pandit Pant Marg, New Delhi 110 001
Tel: 91 11 371 6920 *Fax:* 91 11 371 0803

Ireland (Northern Area): Leprosy House, 44 Ulsterville Avenue,
Belfast BT9 7AQ
Tel: (44) 01232 381937 *Fax:* (44) 01232 381842

Ireland (Southern Area): 5 St James Terrace, Clonskeagh Road, Dublin 6
Tel: (44) 353 126 98804

Italy: Via Rismondo 10A, 05100 Terni
Tel: 39 744 425914 *Fax:* 39 744 409054

Netherlands: Postbus 926, 7301 BD Apeldoorn
Tel: (31) 55 3558535 *Fax:* (31) 55 3554772

New Zealand: PO Box 10-227, Auckland
Tel: 64 9 630 2818 *Fax:* 64 9 630 0784

Portugal: Casa Adelina, sítio do Poio, 8500 Portimão
Tel: 351 82 471180 *Fax:* 351 82 471516

Scotland: 89 Barnton Street, Stirling FK3 1HJ
Tel/Fax: (44) 01786 449266

South-East Asia: PO Box 149, Katong 9143, Singapore
Tel: 65 294 0137 *Fax:* 65 294 7663

South Africa: P Bag X 06, Lyndhurst 2106, Johannesburg
Tel: 27 11 882 6156 *Fax:* 27 11 882 0441

Spain: C/Beneficencia 18 Bis-1°, 28004 Madrid
Tel/Fax: 34 1 5945105

Sweden: Box 145, S-692 23 Kumla
Tel/Fax: 46 19583790

Switzerland: Chemin de Réchoz, 1027 Lonay/VD
Tel: 41 21 8015081 *Fax:* 41 21 8031948

Zimbabwe: PO Box H G 893, Highlands, Harare, Zimbabwe
Tel/Fax: 263 4 721166

Further copies of this book and other titles by the same author may be purchased from your national office.